What Is Chrysalis?

Sharlyn DeHaven Gates

WHAT IS CHRYSALIS?
Copyright © 2003 by Upper Room Books®
All rights reserved.

No part of this book may be reproduced in an any manner whatsoever without written permission of the publisher except in brief quotations in critical articles or reviews. For information, write Upper Room Books, 1908 Grand Avenue, Nashville, TN 37212.

The Upper Room® Web site: www.upperroom.org

Upper Room,® Upper Room Books,® and design logos are trademarks owned by The Upper Room,® Nashville, Tennessee. All rights reserved.

Scripture quotations are from the New Revised Standard Version Bible, copyright © 1989, Division of Christian Education of the National Churches of Christ in the United States of America. Used by permission. All rights reserved.

At the time of publication all Web sites referenced in this book were valid. However, due to the fluid nature of the Internet, some addresses may have changed or the content may no longer be relevant.

Cover Design: Bruce Gore / Gore Studio, Inc.
Interior Design and Implementation: Nancy Cole-Hatcher
First Printing: 2003
ISBN 0-8358-9881-4
Printed in the United States of America

ABOUT THE AUTHOR

Sharlyn DeHaven Gates is pastor, First Presbyterian Church, Parsons, Kansas. She served as International Chrysalis Director for Upper Room Ministries from 2000 to 2003.

Contents

Introduction / 4
What Is Chrysalis? / 6
How Did Chrysalis Begin? / 8
What Is the Purpose of Chrysalis? / 9
Why the Name Chrysalis? / 10
What Happens on a Chrysalis Event? / 10
Who Leads Chrysalis? / 14
Chrysalis Offers Separate-Gender Events / 15
How Do I Attend a Chrysalis Event? / 16
Who Can Attend a Chrysalis Event? / 18
What Will My Experience Be Like? / 20
What Will Be Expected of Me? / 21
What Happens in Next Steps Groups? / 22
What Is an Emmaus/Chrysalis Community? / 22
What Are the Strengths of Chrysalis? / 23
Chrysalis Is Intentional about Follow-up / 25
What Are the Dangers of Chrysalis? / 25
How Can Chrysalis Benefit Churches? / 27
How Can Chrysalis Foster Reconciliation? / 29
What Is The Upper Room? / 31
Summary / 32
Suggested Resources / 33

Introduction

I often hear people say that Chrysalis is a once-in-a-lifetime experience, and, for the most part, I agree. Nevertheless, every time I go back as a team member, I'm transformed all over again.

The Chrysalis weekend is not simply a life-changing event; it is a life-shaping event. I'll never forget the lessons learned and good times had during my first Chrysalis Flight or on weekends when I have been privileged to serve as a team member.

I think the best way to sum up Chrysalis is this: Chrysalis is three days of catching a mere glimpse of God's love. During Chrysalis, love surrounds and fills you, and that is truly a remarkable and spiritual experience!

—*Brandon in Tennessee*

The Chrysalis Flight was a wonderful experience for me. It helped bridge the transition from my childlike faith to the vital and intense spiritual hunger I experience as an adult. I am truly thankful for the hope, encouragement, and guidance I received from other people on my flight.

—*Noelle in Texas*

Chrysalis is a place where young people encounter the living God, where religion becomes more than form—it becomes power. As young people hear adult and youth speakers tell personal stories about the difference God has made in their lives, and as the weekend's events connect with what they have already learned in church, a metamorphosis begins: a transformation from a taught faith to a faith of their own. God's design for their lives begins to be real, and young people often experience a desire to seek the journey to which God calls them. Through Chrysalis, young people become new creations in Christ.

Isaiah 40:30-31 says, "Even youths will faint and be weary, and the young will fall exhausted; but those who wait for the LORD shall renew their strength, they shall mount up with wings like eagles, they shall run and not be weary, they shall walk and not faint."

It is no secret that today's young people face many pressures and uncertainties that may cause them to "faint and be weary." Some of their challenges have been common to every generation: finding their identity, responding to peer pressure, deciding whether to attend college, and discovering future job potential, to name a few. However, now young people must deal with even more daunting problems: communication with parents in spite of overscheduled lives, unstable home lives with the divorce rate at an all-time high, drug and alcohol issues, academic pressures, suicide of friends, school shootings, and the threat of biological and nuclear war.

The Gospel of John proclaims the coming of Christ with this good news: "The light shines in the darkness, and the darkness did not overcome it" (1:5). Yet, in an age that has been described as post-Christian, how do young people experience the Light and the hope that the darkness has not and will not overcome it?

One of the brightest lights of hope in a world that might otherwise look dark to young people is a movement called Chrysalis. Of course, Chrysalis is not the Light itself, but it is a

> *In Chrysalis, a metamorphosis begins for young people: a transformation from a taught faith to a faith of their own.*

means by which the Light not only is seen but also experienced in a new and profound way.

Through Chrysalis, young lives are transformed and God's grace becomes known, resulting in joy, hope, and peace. Young people experience God's powerful gift of the Holy Spirit, which helps them move into the lives God intended for them. Not only do they learn that "the light shines in the darkness," but they become empowered to serve as light to others.

However, Chrysalis is not appropriate for every young person. It is one of many meaningful tools that can develop strong young Christians. Young people who truly desire to grow in the faith and to strengthen their relationship with Jesus Christ will find Chrysalis most helpful.

WHAT IS CHRYSALIS?

> Chrysalis provided me with information and wisdom that has been invaluable in my faith journey—what I learned has helped me through challenges and also inspired and matured my walk with God.
> —*Rosa in Australia*

Chrysalis is an interdenominational, interracial, and international ministry for youth and young adults. Led by adults and young people who have experienced a three-day event, it is offered for two age levels: Chrysalis Flights for youth in grades 10–12, and Chrysalis Journeys for college-age young adults, ages 19–24.

Chrysalis developed in response to numerous requests for a spiritual renewal movement for youth and young adults. Like The Walk to Emmaus, Chrysalis provides a 72-hour "short course" in Christianity during which participants live in Christian community, hear and respond to fifteen talks on God's grace and Christian discipleship, and attend worship services, some of which include celebration of Holy Communion. Prayer undergirds the entire three days—before, during, and after. Chrysalis is the primary outreach program of the Emmaus community. When an Emmaus Board decides to begin a Chrysalis community, it also commits to obey Jesus' command "Go therefore and make disciples" (Matt. 28:19). Together, Emmaus and Chrysalis leaders—youth and adults—join in God's mission of reconciliation, renewal, and transformation.

Each year thousands of young people experience God's transforming love and grace by attending a Chrysalis weekend.

> Many young people testify that they truly came to know Christ for the first time on their Chrysalis event.

Many of them testify that they truly came to know Christ for the first time on their Chrysalis event. Others find new inspiration and insights that cause them to renew their relationship with God and the church. Some even hear a call to ordained ministry through Chrysalis.

Youth and adult members of the Emmaus/Chrysalis community support each three-day event by praying, preparing and serving meals, and performing other acts of love. As in The Walk to Emmaus, males and females attend separate events. Some Chrysalis communities hold concurrent events, conducting the three days for males and females at the same time but using separate leadership teams and conference rooms.

During the Chrysalis weekend, participants meet in small groups to learn, discuss, and pray together. They are encouraged to follow up their Chrysalis weekend by joining a small spiritual support group called a Next Steps group. Members of these groups encourage one another to continue on the journey of discipleship, pray for one another, and hold one another accountable for weekly spiritual commitments.

Both the three-day event and Next Steps groups help renew and strengthen young Christian leaders for the church of Jesus Christ—young people who are leaders now as well as in the future.

> *The purpose of Chrysalis is to support the church's efforts to guide the spiritual formation of young people.*

The Upper Room Chrysalis staff estimates that nearly twenty thousand young people experience Chrysalis each year in 230 sites around the world, including the United States, Costa Rica, Mexico, Puerto Rico, England, South Africa, Germany, and Australia.

How Did Chrysalis Begin?

In 1984, The Upper Room began offering Chrysalis as a youth counterpart to The Walk to Emmaus, a spiritual renewal and leadership development program. The Walk to Emmaus is an adaptation of the Roman Catholic Cursillo (pronounced "cur-SEE-yoh") movement, which started in Spain in 1949. The original Cursillo leaders designed their *Cursillo de Cristianidad* (meaning "short course in Christianity") to empower persons to transform their living and working environments into Christian environments.

What Is the Purpose of Chrysalis?

Chrysalis aims to support the church's efforts to guide the spiritual formation of Christian young people. It provides young people in the church with a course in the essentials of Christian faith and practice that is both educational and experiential. During the three-day course, Chrysalis participants become a Christian community. Together they experience the living Christ through a daily pattern of worship and reflection, systematic teaching and small-group dialogue, creative expression and play, prayer, and signs of support from the wider Chrysalis and Emmaus communities. As a result, young people grow spiritually in a variety of ways that lead to wholeness and increased readiness to live out their Christian discipleship in today's world.

The Chrysalis event calls young people to receive the dynamic friendship God offers through Jesus Christ, to become the unique and beautiful expressions of God's image they were created to be, and to grow together in the grace and love of Jesus Christ as servants of God in church and society. After the three-day experience, Chrysalis encourages young people to share the love they have received; to act as energetic and renewing influences in their churches, youth groups, and schools; and to keep their faith and fire alive by participating in Next Steps groups and occasional gatherings of the entire Chrysalis community.

Chrysalis significantly impacts the spiritual lives of young people and makes a difference in the ecumenical body of Christ.

WHY THE NAME CHRYSALIS?

The butterfly, an ancient Christian symbol of Christ's death and resurrection, provides the central metaphor of the Chrysalis weekend. The life cycle of the butterfly marvelously illustrates the journey of spiritual growth into which Chrysalis invites young people. Beginning life as a caterpillar, the butterfly undergoes an amazing transformation during the chrysalis stage, dying to its old self so that it can become what it is meant to be. Similarly, the process of transformation in Christ involves dying with Christ to the old self through faith in God's accepting love (the focus of Day One), rising with Christ to a new self motivated by hope in God's promise (the focus of Day Two), and going forth with Christ as the church to joyfully share God's ministry of reconciliation and love with an alienated world (the focus of Day Three).

> *The life cycle of the butterfly illustrates the journey of spiritual growth into which Chrysalis invites young people.*

The Chrysalis event helps young people begin to understand and experience what Paul meant when he wrote, "If anyone is in Christ, there is a new creation: everything old has passed away; see, everything has become new!" (2 Cor. 5:17).

WHAT HAPPENS ON A CHRYSALIS EVENT?

I love the layout of the Chrysalis three days, because it encourages you and equips you by modeling Jesus' love, and what better example is there than that?

> Chrysalis was a special time for me because God used it to encourage me and remind me of God's love despite my failures. I really understand grace and faith now and am more thankful for them than ever.
> —*Jaimie, a college student in North Carolina*

> At some time during the three days, the alabaster cast seems to break open. The time comes when a talk becomes more than a talk—the Word becomes flesh and dwells among us.
> —*Clergyperson in North Carolina*

There is no way to describe the richness of the three-day Chrysalis experience. The entire weekend is full of blessings; the event is both fun and deeply meaningful. For many, it is life-changing.

The following schedule outlines the main parts of the weekend, but it also shows the fullness and gives an idea of the purpose of Chrysalis. Studying this schedule can help you see why the event is described as a short course in Christianity rather than as a retreat.

Each of the three days has a particular focus:

Day One calls participants to think about how God created each of them with a unique design and purpose. It invites them to come to know on a deeper level how God loves, forgives, and offers new life in Christ. Day One offers opportunities for participants to consider how they might die with Christ to the old self. This is why, on Day One, participants are called Caterpillars.

Day Two focuses on living in the hope and love of Christ as Christian disciples. This day emphasizes the cocoon stage (the chrysalis), the important time in the butterfly's life cycle when it becomes strong and ready for a new life. The chrysalis stage is the time for growing, preparing to break out of the cocoon, and getting ready

"At some time during the three days, the alabaster cast seems to break open . . . the Word becomes flesh and dwells among us."

to fly. Likewise, on Day Two, the participants learn about important tools for growing as strong disciples—tools like prayer and study—so that they will be ready to go out into the world to serve Christ.

Day Three focuses on the empowerment of the Holy Spirit. This is the day when participants are called Butterflies as they are encouraged to receive God's gifts and to "fly with Christ" in Christian service, making a difference in the church and community by their Christian witness and example.

Here is an overview of the three-day schedule.

Day One: Faith
A Day of Dying with Christ

8:00 A.M. Arrival/Registration
Orientation/Introductions/Group Building
Talk #1: IDEALS
Lunch
Talk #2: GOD DESIGNED YOU
Talk #3: FAITH
Dinner
Worship
Talk #4: GOD LOVES YOU
Talk #5: PRODIGAL
Service of Prayer and Meditation

Day Two: Hope
A Day of Rising with Christ

7:45 A.M. Morning Prayer
Breakfast
Talk #6: COMMUNICATION THROUGH PRAYER
Talk #7: CHRISTIAN GROWTH THROUGH STUDY
Lunch
Talk #8: GOD'S GIFT TO YOU
Holy Communion
Special Dinner
Talk #9: MARRIAGE
Talk #10: GOD SUSTAINS YOU
Special Service of Night Prayer

Day Three: Love
A Day of Flying with Christ

7:30 A.M. Morning Prayer
Talk #11: CHRISTIAN ACTION
Talk #12: SINGLE LIFE
Talk #13: GOD EMPOWERS YOU
Lunch
Talk #14: PRIESTHOOD OF ALL BELIEVERS
Talk #15: NEXT STEPS
Commissioning
Holy Communion and Closing

WHO LEADS CHRYSALIS?

Everybody needs a face that lights up when he or she walks into a room.

—*Author unknown*

One of Chrysalis's greatest strengths is that adults—lay and clergy—lead the program, modeling leadership and discipleship. But equally important is the presence of caring adults who teach by example, listening to and loving the participants, and praying with and for them. In Chrysalis, young people find adult mentors of all ages—adults who value young people and encourage them to give their best. The faces of these adults light up in the presence of young people, demonstrating to them Christ's love and grace. Chrysalis participants often say at Closing, "The best part was the love I felt from people I didn't even know."

Just as important as adult leaders in Chrysalis are young people who have experienced the Chrysalis event. They become invaluable leaders for their peers. Participants find spiritual friends in these young leaders—friends who have grown in their own faith, willingly share their joys and struggles, and make themselves available to talk and pray with participants.

"The best part was the love I felt from people I didn't even know."

While the weekend provides opportunities for participants to develop friendships with everyone in attendance, a special, deep bond usually forms within the small group at each table. Every table group is led by an adult and a young person who have experienced a three-day event and model how to live in Christian community (Eph. 4:2-3).

CHRYSALIS OFFERS SEPARATE-GENDER EVENTS

> I can't imagine my Chrysalis weekend being all that it was if I'd had to worry about girls being there. I could just be myself—pray, talk honestly, even cry when I needed to. It was awesome!
> —*High school student in Pennsylvania*

> I have noticed how much freer the girls are to express thoughts, reactions, and emotions without the presence of boys. I really believe in the separate-gender concept, as I feel that there is much less interruption to the message of the weekend and a greater focus on the specific needs and interests of either girls or boys.
> —*Anna in Australia*

Like The Walk to Emmaus, Chrysalis events are intended to be separate-gender experiences. Chrysalis is designed to help each young person set aside seventy-two hours to focus on his or her relationship with God. At a time in the lives of adolescents and young adults when the opposite gender often serves as a strong distraction, Chrysalis removes this and other distractions to allow young people to give themselves more fully to the experience.

> *Chrysalis removes the distraction of opposite gender to allow young people to give themselves more fully to the weekend.*

Both male and female participants often express gratitude for not having to worry about seeing the opposite sex during their Chrysalis three days, so they could "just be themselves" without concern for how they looked, what they said, or how they acted. Also, the weekend provides an opportunity to develop strong bonds with other Christian young people of the same sex.

After the three-day event, however, young men and women have many opportunities to participate in activities together. Chrysalis offers regularly scheduled gatherings for the entire community (called Hoots), as well as Next Steps groups and opportunities to serve on background teams for future Flights and Journeys. Some communities offer coed retreats for all young people who have attended a three-day event. Chrysalis participants are also welcome to attend Emmaus Gatherings and to serve in many ways on Emmaus Walks.

How Do I Attend a Chrysalis Event?

Chrysalis approaches recruitment differently from many youth ministries—it relies on prayer and sponsorship. Sponsorship, the method for passing the Chrysalis experience from person to person, reflects the way God purposefully reaches out to individuals through other people. After a Chrysalis event, participants naturally want to share the gift of those three days with others. Sponsorship provides them a caring and disciplined way to pass on this experience.

Sponsorship, one of the most important responsibilities in the Emmaus/Chrysalis movement, involves more than simply enlisting youth. Adults and young people who have been through Chrysalis share the responsibility of sponsoring new persons.

Good sponsorship introduces an element of discernment into the recruitment of young people. Discernment means that sponsors actively seek to know and do God's will. Good sponsors do not set out to recruit just anyone willing to attend Chrysalis; instead, they look for young people who seem most ready for the program—those who desire to grow in Christian faith.

After each Chrysalis event, sponsors play an important role in helping their Butterflies return to the real world. They make themselves available to answer Butterflies' questions, to be faithful friends, and to provide perspective. Sponsors guide young people to join follow-up groups (Next Steps), encourage them to renew connections with their churches and youth groups, and help new Butterflies sponsor other youth to attend a Chrysalis three-day event. Sponsors also talk with parents of potential participants and provide transportation and/or financial assistance if needed.

If you are interested in being sponsored or in sponsoring someone to a Chrysalis event, ask a friend who has gone through Chrysalis or an adult who has experienced Emmaus to tell you about his or her experience and how you can be sponsored. If you do not know anyone who might sponsor you, contact The Upper Room's Chrysalis Office for information about Chrysalis in your area. Call toll-free at (877) 899-2780, extension 7229; e-mail

Sponsorship, one of the most important responsibilities in the Emmaus/ Chrysalis movement, reflects the way God purposefully reaches out to individuals through other people.

chrysalis@upperroom.org; or write to the Chrysalis Office, 1908 Grand Avenue, Nashville, TN 37212. Information about sponsorship is also available on The Upper Room Web site: www.upperroom.org/chrysalis.

WHO CAN ATTEND A CHRYSALIS EVENT?

Chrysalis Flights are for young people in high school grades 10–12 (ages 15–18). Chrysalis Journeys are for college-age young people (ages 19–24), but they are not exclusively for college students. Young adults who are out of high school but do not attend college may participate in a Chrysalis Journey.

> *In Chrysalis, young people come to see that they are one in Christ and that their identity transcends racial, cultural, denominational, and economic differences.*

Likely candidates for a Chrysalis event include these:

• *Young people who attend church and youth groups.* Chrysalis is, first and foremost, for young people who are active in their churches. From among them, youth leaders, youth pastors, and adult youth helpers can point out persons who seem ready to grow and to attend an event like Chrysalis. Sponsoring active church youth benefits both the youth and the church. Chrysalis reinforces and vitalizes the faith formation churches already provide for young people.

• *Leaders within the church youth group.* These young leaders will return from Chrysalis bringing infectious energy and vision to their youth group. Their testimony will convince others of the value of participation.

- *Mature youth and leaders on campus.* When campus leaders participate and find meaning in the experience, others want to do likewise. Chrysalis builds upon their natural leadership abilities and calls them to be a positive, Christian influence.
- *Youth with fledgling faith or limited Christian background.* Chrysalis can focus the Christian message for these youth and give them an opportunity to respond to the gospel, perhaps for the first time. But Chrysalis is appropriate for them only when they demonstrate a real desire to know more about Christ and the life of faith.
- *Youth in the church who are not involved in the youth group activities.* Chrysalis can help them connect with other youth and may offer the kind of solid experience they are seeking. But again, they should not be sponsored unless they demonstrate a desire to learn more about the Christian faith.
- *Youth of various races, economic backgrounds, and churches.* In Chrysalis, young people come to see that they are one in Christ and that their true identity transcends racial, cultural, denominational, and economic differences. Breaking out of a closed circle of friends and associations to sponsor different kinds of persons enhances the Chrysalis experience and spreads it to new friendship networks.
- *Friends from school or elsewhere who are not part of the church but show evidence of a desire to meet Christ and to grow spiritually.* Sponsors of these young persons must be committed to connecting them with a church and/or youth group before (if possible) and especially after Chrysalis.

Not everyone will enjoy Chrysalis or find it helpful. The Chrysalis schedule is intense. While the weekend provides many opportunities for fun and fellowship, it is a rigorous, busy seventy-two hours. Some young people simply are not ready for this kind of event.

Chrysalis is not appropriate for young people currently undergoing a crisis or who have recently experienced a trauma. While it may seem that Chrysalis could help them, the risk is that these young people may not be able to fully receive the benefits of the Chrysalis experience, and their needs may distract other participants.

What Will My Experience Be Like?

Each person who attends a Chrysalis Flight or Journey has a somewhat different experience. While everyone hears the same talks and participates in the same activities, Chrysalis affects people in different ways. Some young people return from Chrysalis feeling a stronger desire to live into God's grace for the rest of their lives, wanting to serve as they have been served, and excited about telling others what God has done for them. They return to their churches and youth groups with new vitality and passion. For others, the changes may not be that evident. Chrysalis may plant a seed that continues growing in them as they think during the coming weeks about what they learned and experienced. Chrysalis may be one of many steps on the faith journey that eventually brings them to a decision to live as a faithful disciple. Still others may leave the three days feeling good about the new friendships they developed, while a few will just be glad the weekend is over.

The aim of Chrysalis is to encourage the spiritual formation of young people and to develop strong leaders for the church—both now and in the future. How the Holy Spirit accomplishes that purpose varies from person to person. However, many young people have given testimony that, with the help of Chrysalis, they have experienced a stronger call to discipleship, a new love for God, an understanding of the power of the Holy Spirit in their lives, and a sense of truly being transformed through new life in Christ.

What Will Be Expected of Me?

Be yourself. You will not be asked to do anything that will embarrass you. You will not be expected to know a great deal about the Bible or to act like a saint. You will be respected and cared for just as you are. All the Chrysalis team expects of you is that you be honest, fully participate, and respond with authenticity and sincerity to the message heard each day.

Come with openness to the message of the Chrysalis Flight/Journey. Remain open to others and to God.

Be present for the entire seventy-two hours. If you cannot be present for the whole time, it would be best to postpone attending an event. Each part of the Chrysalis experience is important and plays a role in conveying the overall message. Each person who attends becomes an indispensable member of the three-day community and of his or her table group.

Leave your world behind for the three days. Chrysalis provides a time apart with God. You are asked to leave behind homework, projects, phones, electronic games, and other distractions in order to give your full attention to the Chrysalis experience.

What Happens in Next Steps Groups?

Ideally, after a Chrysalis event, young people will find a small group of peers to meet with regularly. Most Next Steps groups meet once a week for an hour, sharing with one another the strengths and weaknesses of their Christian walk since their last meeting. Group members encourage one another and pray together. Each person receives a Next Steps card on Day Three of the Chrysalis event, and groups use the pattern on this card to guide their meeting.

First, all group members review their prayer life and reflect on how they have nourished their relationship with God and when they felt closest to Christ in the past week. Second, group members share how their study time went, reflecting on how they worked on cultivating the mind of Christ in themselves and what they are doing to better understand the Christian life in the world. Third, group members talk about what they are doing to reach others for Christ. Each person is then invited to share plans for supporting and participating in the ministry of his or her church during the following week. The meeting concludes with prayer.

Next Steps groups sometimes consist of young people at the same church or youth group. Youth who have not yet experienced a Chrysalis Flight or Journey are welcome to participate in Next Steps groups. Some groups prefer to limit themselves to one gender, while others are coed.

What Is an Emmaus/Chrysalis Community?

An Emmaus/Chrysalis community consists of all the persons in a geographic area who have attended a Walk to

Emmaus or a Chrysalis Flight or Journey. The community meets regularly, usually once a month, to celebrate God's grace, to support one another, and to keep alive the enthusiasm for living in God's love and grace. Some Emmaus/Chrysalis communities meet together first as a large group, and then Chrysalis breaks off for a different meeting. Others have completely separate gatherings. Emmaus refers to its community meetings as Gatherings. Chrysalis usually refers to its meetings as Hoots; however, they also may be called Gatherings. Each Emmaus community relies on local leadership, an elected Board of Directors. Chrysalis also depends on elected local leaders who are a standing committee of the Emmaus Board. Each group of leaders signs a separate Letter of Agreement with The Upper Room and covenants to operate within the guidelines of the program. The Upper Room provides resources and training to support the ongoing development of the programs. Every person who has participated in a three-day experience becomes a potential leader in the Emmaus/Chrysalis movement.

WHAT ARE THE STRENGTHS OF CHRYSALIS?

Chrysalis is a place of continued community, support, and Christian growth. Since its beginning, thousands of youth and young adults around the world have experienced this wonderful ministry God has used to renew and strengthen their faith and to develop strong Christian leaders for the ecumenical body of Christ.

Chrysalis fosters deep and lasting friendships. Relationships are important in Chrysalis. The three-day events provide time to form long-lasting friendships that are often life-shaping—relationships based on a shared experience of Christian love, faith, and growth. The design of the Chrysalis event and follow-up (Next Steps groups, Hoots, and Gatherings) encourages these new friendships. These bonds of friendship continue to strengthen naturally through frequent letters or e-mails, telephone conversations, and messages passed through mutual friends.

Chrysalis offers role models and mentors. Chrysalis fosters positive relationships among young people and mature Christian adults who can provide support and guidance long after the three-day experience. This is one of the most vital aspects of the Chrysalis program.

> *One of the great strengths of Chrysalis is that wherever there is a Chrysalis community, the program remains consistent and trustworthy.*

Chrysalis develops leadership skills in young people. Both during their three-day experience and through participation on teams and follow-up activities, young people discover new gifts for self-expression; learn to exercise their gifts in self-giving ways that enrich the Chrysalis/Emmaus community; and experience affirmation for who they are and for growing into their God-given potential.

One of the great strengths of Chrysalis is that wherever there is a Chrysalis community, the program is essentially the same. Even though the culture may be different and certainly the adults and young people all bring a fresh, new element to the three days, the program remains consistent and trustworthy. A young person can e-mail, phone, or meet someone from another country who has experienced Chrysalis and talk about the program with some certainty that the other young person will understand.

Chrysalis Is Intentional about Follow-up

From the outset Chrysalis is designed to be more than just a mountaintop experience. Chrysalis offers follow-up opportunities aimed at strengthening young people's relationships with one another in the faith and at supporting their growth as disciples of Jesus Christ through the church. Chrysalis spiritual support groups (Next Steps groups) provide a way for Butterflies to keep alive the fire of faith in their hearts; to encourage one another in daily prayer, study, and action; and to benefit from faithful friendships by sharing one another's struggles and joys. Hoots provide a setting for young people and adults to share their faith, identify ways they are carrying out commitments made during the Chrysalis event, have fun, and celebrate God's grace in their lives.

What Are the Dangers of Chrysalis?

> No one puts new wine into old wineskins; otherwise, the wine will burst the skins, and the wine is lost, and so are the skins.
> —*Mark 2:22*

When young people return to their churches after a Chrysalis event where they have experienced the joy of adults and youth, clergy and laypeople, working together effectively in ministry, they are eager to replicate this experience in their local community of faith. They are like "new wine."

One of the greatest dangers of Chrysalis is also a great strength. Chrysalis aims to renew young people spiritually so that they will become hungry and eager to serve. If they return to their local congregations and find adults closed to their participation, unwilling to listen to their young voices, or pastors and youth leaders who do not understand what the Chrysalis experience has meant to them, they can become disappointed and frustrated. If young people do not have a place within their own churches to live out the calling to be the church—to be new wine—the danger is that the wine will be lost. Young people will find other ways to answer the call.

If young people do not have a place within their churches to live out the calling to be the church—to be new wine—the danger is that the "wine" will be lost.

Sponsors, pastors, and parents must be well informed about Chrysalis before a young person attends. After the event they need to make available opportunities for the continued spiritual growth of the young person.

The Upper Room Handbook on Chrysalis provides sample letters for sponsors to send to the parents and the pastor of each young person they sponsor. Good sponsors will do all they can to ensure that people close to the young person understand the Chrysalis event and will build on the spiritual renewal that has begun during the three days.

How Can Chrysalis Benefit Churches?

> Chrysalis changed the way I thought about my value to my congregation. I realized that all I had to do was say yes, and God would equip me for the specific job he had for me. I then had the confidence, desire, and ability to serve in a range of new ways, such as music, youth group, and leadership positions.
> —*Anna in Australia*

An Iowa pastor tells the story of organizing a youth group within her small, rural congregation:

> We started out with a ten-minute devotion time, which the youth seemed to tolerate at best. They enjoyed the fellowship, eating supper together every Sunday night, playing games that strengthened their bond with one another, and singing songs—some of them spiritual but many of them fun, camp songs. After a year of meeting this way, something wonderful happened: A couple of our youth were sponsored to attend a Chrysalis weekend.
>
> Those two young people, a young man and a young woman, returned from their weekend very different. They couldn't stop talking about God's love and about the experience and their new desire to live differently. Those two young people sponsored two more youth, and so it went until most of the youth group had participated in Chrysalis. The whole youth group was transformed!
>
> I began taking commentaries and other books to our meetings to help answer questions our young people asked. Soon the youth refused to sing songs that were not Christian. They organized a prayer group that met each morning outside the school, with others gradually joining them throughout the school year. They initiated a prayer time for a member who was

having a serious surgery; each of them laid hands on her and prayed for her.

Not only was our youth group changed, but our congregation also changed. New life was evident in our worship services as young people sang special music, led liturgy, and wrote and acted in skits. The pews were filled with young people who showed real interest in hearing the Word preached. They also planned mission projects and led Vacation Bible School.

The youth meeting that had started out just as a fellowship time became an important priority. Also, what began as a small group from our congregation ended up being very ecumenical, with youth from the Roman Catholic tradition and several Protestant churches joining in. For our congregation, Chrysalis was a true gift of new life in Christ!

In recent years many churches have noticed a decline in the number of their youth and young adults. Some smaller congregations lack the resources and leadership necessary to carry on the ministry and mission of the church. Still other congregations lack vitality and enthusiasm.

Like The Walk to Emmaus, Chrysalis is designed to develop leaders, deepen their faith, and revitalize their sense of calling to be the salt of the earth and the light of the world (Matt. 5:13-14). The Holy Spirit works through Chrysalis to awaken in young people a love and passion for God and to encourage them to live into the new life Christ offers. This spiritual renewal causes young people to bring enthusiasm and a genuine desire to grow and serve as they attend worship services, youth activities, and small-group studies. When young people gain new visions of what it means to be the body of Christ, the whole congregation can find itself suddenly alive and growing, with a new vision and sense of mission.

Church leaders willing to allow youth participation often find Chrysalis young people eager to lead in worship services, Vacation Bible School, Bible studies, mission projects, and so on. It is often said that youth are the leaders of the future. While that statement is true, it is important to realize that God also equips youth with the gifts and desire to serve as leaders now.

Young people come away from the Chrysalis experience with a deeper understanding of and hunger for Holy Communion, fellowship with other Christians, Bible study, and opportunities to serve.

How Can Chrysalis Foster Reconciliation?

Because Chrysalis is international, interracial, and interdenominational, it reaches across walls that sometime divide and cause hostility. Chrysalis offers a place to learn about and experience God's love and grace, which Gods extends to all. It is a setting where young people of different denominations and diverse races and cultures have opportunities to join together and learn tolerance and love for one another.

Chrysalis fosters reconciliation between each young person and God. No healing is so sweet a balm as the experience of God's amazing grace and forgiveness flooding into a wounded heart. As with the story of the prodigal son, many young people feel they have wandered to their own "far country." To hear the words that

> *It is often said that youth are the leaders of the future. While that statement is true, it is also important to realize that God equips youth with gifts and the desire to serve as leaders now.*

the loving Father longs for them to come home, welcomes them with open arms, and celebrates their homecoming with great joy is, in itself, to be given new life, a new beginning, a second chance! Young people remain very much aware of their need to "come home" and long for an opportunity to do so. Chrysalis offers them this opportunity throughout the weekend in a loving and nonmanipulative way.

> *Young people remain very much aware of their need to "come home" and long for an opportunity to do so. Chrysalis offers them this opportunity throughout the weekend in a loving and nonmanipulative way.*

Chrysalis fosters reconciliation among young people, their parents, and other adults. Most young people want to be known and understood. They desire sincere relationships with adults characterized by mutual respect and genuine care. The "generation gap" seems to narrow as young people experience God's love for them and as they work together with adults in Chrysalis, discovering their unity in Christ. As Ephesians 2 puts it so well, "[Christ] has broken down the dividing wall, that is, the hostility between us. . . . So then you are no longer strangers and aliens, but you are citizens with the saints and also members of the household of God . . . with Christ Jesus himself as the cornerstone" (vv. 14, 19-20).

This kind of reconciliation stretches beyond families into churches, schools, and communities. When young people are affirmed in who and whose they are in Christ

Jesus, they often take the initiative to approach adults and offer friendship. But often, adults see something new (could it be the light of Christ?) and are drawn toward those bright young faces. For some youth, Chrysalis offers their first extended time of learning, serving, worshiping, and praying with members of other denominations who are their age and gender. Chrysalis provides a positive foundation for youth to experience firsthand the body of Christ at work in love and service.

What Is The Upper Room?

Most people know The Upper Room through *The Upper Room* daily devotional guide. In addition to that magazine, The Upper Room publishes many other resources designed to encourage Christian spiritual formation, and it offers leadership development and spiritual renewal programs opportunities such as The Walk to Emmaus, Chrysalis, Companions in Christ, and the Academy for Spiritual Formation. Chrysalis is a copyrighted program of The Upper Room.

The Upper Room is part of the General Board of Discipleship of The United Methodist Church, an agency that provides resources and consultation for local churches. The Upper Room's mission is to provide resources that help people grow in their relationship with God. The Upper Room's hope is that its ministries will foster networks of people throughout the world who are linked in prayer, who walk together into a vision of new life in Christ, and who share their stories of God. The ministries of The Upper Room are interdenominational, interracial, and international.

Though organizationally part of a funded agency of The United Methodist Church, The Upper Room is unique because of its self-supporting nature. Church offerings do not fund The Upper Room. The Upper Room's ministries depend on proceeds from the sale of resources and from the gifts of donors.

The Upper Room supports Emmaus and Chrysalis by providing a small staff of full-time workers who help start new Emmaus and Chrysalis communities, lead training events, write resources, foster communication among Emmaus/Chrysalis groups, and strive to improve these programs.

SUMMARY

Though Chrysalis is not the only way to experience new life in Christ or God's love, grace, and forgiveness, it certainly is one channel through which the Holy Spirit works today. Thousands of young people each year discover spiritual renewal through the gift of Chrysalis.

Through Chrysalis, we can say with Isaiah, "But those who wait for the LORD shall renew their strength, they shall mount up with wings like eagles, they shall run and not be weary, they shall walk and not faint" (40:31).

Chrysalis is indeed a channel where God pours out His Spirit, where young people discover their wings and are strengthened so they can "fly with Christ"!

Suggested Resources

To order books listed in this section, call
(800) 972-0433 from within the U.S. or Canada,
or visit us online at www.upperroom.org/bookstore.

For Youth and Young Adults

WAY TO LIVE: Christian Practices for Teens
EDITED BY DOROTHY C. BASS AND DON C. RICHTER
Written by a team of teens and adults, *Way to Live* explores concrete ways youth can practice Christianity in everyday life. This book answers teens' yearning for a more meaningful spiritual life by inviting them into the abundant way of life Jesus offers and challenging them to join others in practicing their faith.
ISBN 0-8358-0975-7 • Paperback • 310 pages

COMPELLED TO WRITE TO YOU:
Letters on Faith, Love, Service, and Life
BY CHRISTOPHER DE VINCK AND ELIZABETH M. MOSBO VERHAGE
At pivotal points in our lives, we long for a friend who will hear us and guide us through our questions and doubts. In *Compelled to Write to You*, readers will find that kind of listening in the correspondence between a college senior and a nationally known author. This book is especially helpful for young adults who are searching for spiritual truth.
ISBN 0-8358-0940-4 • Hardcover • 184 pages

GOD GOES TO COLLEGE: Living Faith on Campus
BY HELEN R. NEINAST AND THOMAS C. ETTINGER
This book of 42 essays provides a guide for prayer and reflection, personal devotion, or group study. *God Goes to College* serves a a companion to young adults trying to make sense of life, college, and vocational choices.
ISBN 0-8358-0987-0 • Paperback • 128 pages

WITH HEART AND MIND AND SOUL: A Guide to Prayer for College Students and Young Adults
BY HELEN R. NEINAST AND THOMAS C. ETTINGER
A great gift for high school seniors and college students, *With Heart and Mind and Soul* contains 36 weeks of devotions on relevant topics for young adults, offering ample space for journaling and reflection.
ISBN 0-8358-0695-2 • Paperback • 240 pages

WHAT ABOUT GOD? NOW THAT YOU'RE OFF TO COLLEGE: A Prayer Guide
BY HELEN R. NEINAST AND THOMAS C. ETTINGER
Amid the often confusing transition from high school to college, *What About God?* helps students discern the presence of God in the changes, challenges, and opportunities that confront them. It provides a wonderful introduction to a devotional discipline.
ISBN 0-8358-0655-3 • Paperback/Spiral • 240 pages

SOUL TENDING: Life-Forming Practices for Older Youth and Young Adults
VARIOUS AUTHORS
Expanding on the ideas Kenda Creasy Dean and Ron Foster put forth in *The Godbearing Life*, *Soul Tending* offers a practical way for senior high youth and young adults to study spiritual disciplines while strengthening relationships.
ISBN 0-6870-3079X• Paperback • 192 pages

NOTE: To order *Soul Tending*, call Abingdon Press at 1-800-251-3320, or order online at www.abingdonpress.com.

For Leaders of Youth and Young Adults

THE GODBEARING LIFE:
The Art of Soul Tending for Youth Ministry
BY KENDA CREASY DEAN AND RON FOSTER

Specifically designed to nurture the spiritual life of the youth leader, this spiritual primer is a practical guide for those who pastor young people. With soul-searing honesty, Dean and Foster rechart a course for youth ministry through the classical spiritual disciplines of the church.

ISBN 0-8358-0858-0 • Paperback • 224 pages

CREATING A LIFE WITH GOD:
The Call of Ancient Prayer Practices
BY DANIEL WOLPERT

This book introduces readers to 12 prayer practices—*lectio divina*, the Jesus Prayer, the examen, journaling, body prayer, and praying in nature, among others. Each chapter focuses on a "traveling companion" from history, like Ignatius and Julian of Norwich—individuals and groups who illuminate the prayer practices. An appendix offers step-by-step instructions for practicing the Jesus Prayer and the prayer of examen, for walking the labyrinth, for praying with the body, and more.

ISBN 0-8358-9855-5 • Paperback • 192 pages

OPENING TO GOD:
Guided Imagery Meditation on Scripture
by Carolyn Stahl Bohler

Designed for groups or individuals, *Opening to God* includes 50 guided imagery meditations that will help enhance readers' devotional lives as it allows them to experience God through scripture-based imagination.

ISBN 0-8358-0768-1 • Paperback • 192 pages

SERVANTS, MISFITS, AND MARTYRS: Saints and Their Stories
BY JAMES C. HOWELL

Discover a world of saints whose faith, hope, and action will inspire and encourage you. Meet misfits Francis of Assisi and Clarence Jordan; experience the stories of Sojourner Truth and John Chrysostom; hear the stories of singing saints Charles Wesley, Isaac Watts, and John Newton; read the accounts of prisoners Thomas More and Dietrich Bonhoeffer.

ISBN 0-8358-0906-4 • Paperback •192 pages

CALMING THE RESTLESS SPIRIT: A Journey toward God
BY BEN CAMPBELL JOHNSON

For those seeking a closer relationship with God, Johnson offers nurture and practical guidance for finding meaning in life. The book focuses on how to pray, the significance of scripture and worshiping with others, and how to open our lives to God.

ISBN 0-8358-0814-9 • Paperback •144 pages

HEART WHISPERS: Benedictine Wisdom for Today
BY ELIZABETH J. CANHAM

Using Benedictine spirituality, the author gives readers insights and help with faithful living and balance in today's stressful world. This 10-session study offers exercises for group reflection and for prayerful reading of scripture.

ISBN 0-8358-0892-0 • Paperback •176 pages

SPIRITUAL PREPARATION FOR CHRISTIAN LEADERSHIP
BY E. GLENN HINSON

Hinson presents a vision of "living saints" as the model of spiritual leadership for the church—people who have experienced God's grace in their lives and willingly yield themselves to God. Such a vision creates a new understanding of ways in which the church can be transformed.

ISBN 0-8358-0888-2 • Paperback • 208 pages

FEED MY SHEPHERDS: Spiritual Healing and Renewal for Those in Christian Leadership
BY FLORA SLOSSON WUELLNER
By looking at the intense, healing relationship between the risen Christ and his disciples, Wuellner offers a new paradigm of healing for lay and clergy in caregiving ministries.
ISBN 0-8358-0845-9 • Hardcover • 192 pages

WHERE THE HEART LONGS TO GO: A New Image for Pastoral Ministry
BY THAD RUTTER JR.
Through this book, church leaders can gain awareness of their own spiritual hunger and learn about imaginative ways to help others grow in their faith journey.
ISBN 0-8358-0849-1 • Paperback • 128 pages

Web Sites

METHOD X (the way of Christ) *(For young adults)*
www.methodx.net

DĒVO'ZINE *(For youth, ages 12–18)*
www.devozine.org

CHRYSALIS
www.upperroom.org/chrysalis

WAY TO LIVE: Christian Practices for Teens
www.waytolive.org

THE WALK TO EMMAUS
www.upperroom.org/emmaus

UPPER ROOM BOOKSTORE
www.upperroom.org/bookstore

I LEAD YOUTH *(A Cokesbury Web Site for Youth Leaders)*
www.ileadyouth.com

Emmaus/Chrysalis Resources

SPIRITUAL DIRECTORS
BY KAY GRAY

This book offers helpful advice for Spiritual Directors in The Walk to Emmaus/Chrysalis, covering such topics as the role of Spiritual Directors, qualifications, and responsibilities before, during, and after the three-day event.

ISBN 0-8358-0886-6 • Paperback • 40 pages

WHAT IS EMMAUS?
BY STEPHEN D. BRYANT

This informative book is designed for persons interested in learning more about The Walk to Emmaus. It addresses frequently asked questions about Emmaus.

ISBN 0-8358-0881-5 • Paperback • 40 pages

THE EARLY HISTORY OF THE WALK TO EMMAUS
BY BOB WOOD

The founding International Director of The Walk to Emmaus writes about the early days of the movement. This booklet includes a timeline of significant events in the Emmaus movement.

ISBN 08358-0962-5 • Paperback • 48 pages

COMING DOWN FROM THE MOUNTAIN: Returning to Your Congregation
BY LAWRENCE MARTIN

Martin guides new pilgrims on how to "come down from the mountain and work in the valleys" of everyday congregational life.

ISBN 0-8358-0882-3 • Paperback • 56 pages

WALKING SIDE BY SIDE: Devotions for Pilgrims
BY JOANNE BULTEMEIER AND CHERIE JONES
This book of 45 meditations helps readers reconsider the impact of the Emmaus weekend and continue the daily disciplines of prayer and meditation.
ISBN 0-8358-0880-7 • Paperback • 56 pages

THE GROUP REUNION
BY STEPHEN D. BRYANT
Designed for persons who have participated in The Walk to Emmaus, this book explains the follow-up practice of the Group Reunion.
ISBN 0-8358-0884-X • Paperback • 40 pages

SPONSORSHIP
BY RICHARD AND JANINE GILMORE
Gives guidance to those who wish to sponsor others on The Walk to Emmaus.
ISBN 0-8358-0873-4 • Paperback • 40 pages

MUSIC DIRECTORS
BY SANDY STICKNEY
This book provides helpful instructions for music leaders following the Emmaus and Chrysalis model, giving practical insights on topics ranging from ego to copyright requirements.
ISBN 0-8358-0911-0 • Paperback • 56 pages

SPIRITUAL GROWTH THROUGH TEAM EXPERIENCE
BY JOANNE BULTEMEIER
Drawing on her experience as a team member, Bultemeier covers qualities of a team member, spiritual benefits of team membership, what happens at team meetings, leadership development, and other aspects of being part of an Emmaus team.
ISBN 0-8358-0885-8 • Paperback • 40 pages

THE BOARD OF DIRECTORS
BY RICHARD A. GILMORE

This books explains the responsibilities of board members, duties of board committees, possible committee assignments, and more.

ISBN 0-8358-0883-1 • Paperback • 40 pages

The following publications are available only to Emmaus/Chrysalis communities from The Upper Room.

SUSTAINING THE SPIRIT: A Personal Guide to the Ministry of The Walk to Emmaus for Members of Emmaus Teams BY WILLIAM F. GUSY **#E39**

CHRYSALIS DIRECTORS' MANUAL #C60

CHRYSALIS COORDINATORS' MANUAL #C62

CHRYSALIS TEAM MANUAL #C59

CHRYSALIS TALK OUTLINES #C76

CHRYSALIS THREE-DAY SCHEDULE #C65

THE UPPER ROOM HANDBOOK ON CHRYSALIS #C77

KITCHEN MANUAL #E15